ALLEN LANE
A PERSONAL PORTRAIT

ALLEN LANE
A PERSONAL PORTRAIT

W. E. WILLIAMS

THE BODLEY HEAD
LONDON SYDNEY
TORONTO

To my god-daughter,
Clare Morpurgo,
eldest daughter of
Allen Lane

CONTENTS

ILLUSTRATIONS

I

A SILHOUETTE

I

A SILHOUETTE

It could be said of Allen Lane, as of Christopher
Wren, 'If you seek his monument—look around you.'
Every bookstall in Britain displays the symbol of the
publishing revolution he launched in 1935, when he
was thirty-two, and led for another thirty-five years
until his death in the summer of 1970. It was a silent
revolution sustained by no drum-beating, no pressur-
ized sales campaigns, no competitive gimmicks, not
even by market research. One of the significant phe-
nomena of the Penguin impact was that in the 'thirties
and 'forties relatively little money was spent on pro-
motion. The same is true of Marks and Spencer, a
firm which on a much larger scale has some resem-
blances to Penguin. Massive sums are employed to sell
pet foods, to persuade us to go by air, to take the
family to holiday camps, to adopt a new brand of
whatever we eat or drink or smoke. But none of the
devices of mass persuasion was used to make the
Penguin image familiar and acceptable in its formative
years. It is true, of course, that for all its prestige the
Penguin operation is a minor one in size and scope, but
even measured on its own scale it demonstrates the
reassuring fact that a large market can be won by a
product which depends on its own excellence and on
the discernment of a sufficient sector of the public to
make it profitable. In the last two decades Penguin's

have had to fight to retain their leadership in paperbacks, but even then they have relied less on advertising than on attractive exhibitions and Penguin Weeks in bookshops.

What was the nature of the man who conceived the Penguin enterprise and conducted it so successfully? Before I attempt to answer this question I should describe briefly the basis on which our relationship developed over a period of thirty-five years. I had a close connexion with Penguin's for most of that time but I was never a member of the staff, although on several occasions Allen pressed me to become one. I worked a good deal for the firm but in a strictly extramural capacity and virtually for out-of-pocket expenses. For many years, until 1960, I was the Chief Editor, but never did I have a service agreement or contract of any kind (nor did most of the early series editors). I thus retained at all times a position of detachment and independence which secured me two valuable advantages: I enjoyed special terms of confidence with Allen and I was immune from the tensions which arise among senior management. There were two reasons why I adopted and always maintained this position. The first was my involvement in other activities which were not only remunerative but were also more significant to me even than Penguin's, such as running the Army Bureau of Current Affairs (ABCA) in the war, and later the Arts Council. The second reason was my deep conviction that Allen, who became my closest friend, could well become too invasive and exacting with people whose services he bought. It was on this basis of independence, then, that I was able to assume and preserve a rôle which brought me so close—but never too close—to this brilliant and unpredictable innovator.

A Complicated Character

Allen Lane was a baffling character. Neither his qualities nor his deficiencies were readily apparent—a fact which obviously preoccupied that excellent artist Bryan Kneale in the portrait of Allen Lane he was commissioned to paint in 1960. I might illustrate this point by comparing Allen with such a figure as the late Lord Reith, another notable mass-communicator. In Lord Reith's appearance and conversation the salient characteristics were rapidly and plainly revealed—resolution, conviction, deep-rooted principle, ambition, inflexibility, durability. No one endeavouring to 'read' Allen in this way could compile a summary of his characteristics, for they were, in Shakespeare's phrase, 'of the chameleon's dish'. Because he was gay, volatile, insecure, capricious and unreliable he revealed a bewildering quick-change habit of mind. His capacity to do a mental somersault about a person or a problem no doubt sometimes extricated him from a precarious situation or a dubious decision, but it was a habit which could be the despair of his associates. And when he had wrong-footed a colleague in this way he never expressed a particle of contrition. Even when he contradicted himself in word or deed he reserved the right to have it both ways.

Allen was not much guided by reason. When he said, as he so often did, that he had a hunch about something or someone he was depending on intuition. Now intuition can often produce the right solution but it is not as reliable a compass as those who go by it are inclined to believe. It often led Allen completely astray, and the extent to which he employed it in reaching decisions gave him a reputation for wayward and irresponsible behaviour. This was particularly true of his efforts to recruit people for senior management in the firm. He would sometimes appoint a man impulsively, on meagre evidence of merit, and within a few weeks would be picking holes in the poor fellow and confiding his doubts, as often as not, to the inadequate man's colleagues. There were consequently periods when staff morale was overcast and friction was rife.

A Gift of Curiosity

I remember sitting one day in the office of one of his senior managers, a sardonic character, at a time when a new building was being put up. Our conversation was punctuated by the heavy thuds of a pile-driver and after a time my companion said, 'It sounds as though Allen is practising on his guillotine!' There were times, indeed, when heads rolled with distressing frequency, and the executions were not always just. Many good men came to grief through Allen's summary and capricious decisions. But his habit of hasty and superficial judgement was rectified by other qualities. He had a gift of curiosity which made him ask people questions. His curiosity covered a wide front and was by no means confined to business matters. He put questions to almost everyone he met. One heard him at it anywhere and everywhere, even in the club or at a cocktail party. Not only were his questions always to the point but he was an attentive listener as well and thus evoked a ready and sympathetic response from those whose knowledge and opinion he sought. He had a listening face. He never pretended, as some successful people do, that he knew all the answers, and he made his enquiries with modesty and eagerness. He was in this way a sincere and habitual gleaner of knowledge, so that he was able over and over again to follow a course of action which he would not have discovered by his own unaided confrontation of a problem. It was not that he swallowed advice, for when he received it he relied again on an intuitive ability to decide whether it was right or wrong. Much of his success, as he was the first to agree, depended on this typical practice of consultation and enquiry. He seldom tried to discuss a topic systematically, at length, for he was not logical, but he was an inveterate and diligent quizzer.

The Quality of Bonhomie

Another quality which stood Allen in good stead was his bonhomie. My immediate and predominant memory of him is of a good companion. He was fun most of the time. An evening with him was a gay, light-hearted occasion. The conversation would usually include a generous amount of small talk, for he always relished gossip. He took a particular delight in anecdotes about people we knew who had been involved in some absurd episode. He shared the opinion of the cynical Chinese sage Kai-Lung—'There is no spectacle more agreeable than to observe an old friend fall from a roof-top.' He was exuberant, impish and genially malicious, and the enjoyment he obviously felt at being with an old friend was immediately compulsive. He was never pompous or boring. Thomas Carlyle wrote that men could be separated into those who say 'Nay' to life and those who say 'Yea': nay-sayers and yea-sayers. Allen was emphatically a yea-sayer. He had an eager and consistent appetite for living, a natural effervescence.

I remember hundreds of his visits to my office. He never came straight in but used to put his head round the door first, eyebrows raised enquiringly and a smile at the ready in his vivid blue eyes. After this moment of inspection he would come briskly in and start talking in his rapid staccato manner, jacket buttoned up, as always, and a quick pull at the knot of his tie. He always looked uncomfortable sitting down and preferred to walk about the room as he talked. He needed no prompting, and one was immediately conscious of a warm and friendly temperament, forthcoming and confiding. He filled his diary with lunch and dinner dates and was always good value—except when he was just back from one of his frequent visits to some health farm or other. From these excursions he invariably returned a few pounds lighter but sadly diminished in spirits. A 'cure' was not much good to a man of his ebullience. There was, incidentally, a hypochondriac strain in Allen. Although he enjoyed normal good health most of his life he had bouts of worrying about minor ailments. From time to time, too, he had a weight problem to contend with, and he sometimes tackled this with excessive fervour. Some of his dietary exercises bordered on the bizarre. He liked drink, too, and really needed it, but there were long periods when he went off spirits and drank vast quantities of white wine instead. Hospitable though he always was, he sometimes attempted to persuade one to follow his example, because, perhaps, he felt a bit self-conscious about his abstinence. On the other hand, after long spells of wine-drinking he would break out with characteristic impulsiveness and get back to his favourite dry martinis.

A Man of Few Interests

He had few interests outside his firm and his friends. He played no games, indoor or outdoor, and never watched them either, even on television. For a few months before the Second World War he joined a yeomanry regiment in order, he said, to get free riding, but his ardour soon evaporated. For a brief period he was tempted by his younger brothers, Dick and John, to join them messing about in boats but this momentary interest, too, soon lapsed. Although Allen became a dedicated publisher he read very little, either for personal or business motives, and he knew virtually nothing about literature, even about the writing of his own time. He picked up a lot about books and their authors without actually reading them, and in this respect he was unique among all the publishers I have known. Here again he relied upon questioning friends and colleagues to put him in the picture.

There have been publishers who, like Allen, left school at an early age but set themselves to make up for lost time by voracious reading or attending courses in further education. From the time he left school at the age of sixteen Allen did nothing to cultivate his mind or enlarge his knowledge. He went straight into a publisher's office, learned the trade the hard way, got to the top of the tree and died a millionaire. He tried, without much success, to explore the arts, but he was handicapped by knowing nothing about any of them and not having any natural taste for them. The Aldwych farce was his preference in the theatre, and he lacked even a nodding acquaintance with music of any kind.

He had a quality possessed by many who have won success and power. He was single-minded in his determination to build an empire: single-minded and, in a sense, simple-minded, for he was not troubled or distracted by considerations which give pause to some people pursuing success. Once he became an apprentice to John Lane at The Bodley Head in 1919 he determined to be a publisher and never had a second thought about it, even when he ran into trouble as the subsequent boss of The Bodley Head. His stubborn will gave him a power of perseverance which a more pliant nature would have lacked. He really learned his trade and went about it thoroughly. He got about, he called on booksellers assiduously, and mastered every detail of the business. He 'slogged' for many years as a young man, so that when he decided to go it alone he knew how to do it.

Powers of Persuasion

He was always at immense pains to recognize how much his early success depended on a few men and women who served him as advisers and editors. He was lucky in the early years. He attracted some brilliant collaborators, not for money certainly, for the fees they got were peanuts. He had a great power, almost mesmeric at times, of persuading people to join him. He could be artful, of course, and could shrewdly assess what kind of approach or appeal would go down best with someone he wanted to bring into the circle. Allen came of Devonshire and Welsh farming stock and he was a peasant in many ways: wily, opportunist, unscrupulous, and these traits were often revealed in the way he went about things. One of his favourite books was *The Adventures of Tom Sawyer*, and I often heard him relate the episode which appealed to him immensely and which, of course, matched an element in his own nature. Tom has been ordered by his father to whitewash a fence. This command gives Tom no joy, for it is a fine day and he wants to play with his chums. But as he gets to work he sees that some of the lads have gathered round to watch, and soon one of them asks to have a go. 'All right,' says Tom, 'give me a dime and you can have the brush.' The others soon want to join in and presently Tom is sitting under a tree counting his profits. It was just the trick to appeal to Allen—and he sometimes ran his firm on a similar basis. He was adept at taking advantage of the unwary.

Unspoilt by Success

Wealth and success did not seem to change Allen at all. He was never ostentatious, never interested in the fashionable life nor the trappings of the rich. He certainly enjoyed a social life but never sought companionship outside his own familiar circle. He was good company at a party but he never set the table in a roar nor broached a lively discussion. He was simply a cordial presence and a willing and contented participant. He would sometimes behave oddly, even when he was the host. I remember often, when the drink was having its effect, he would leave the table and his guests and take himself off to bed. He seldom let anything interfere with his convenience. He was an infuriatingly unpunctual person, both in business and social engagements, but he never seemed to mind if other people were late for an appointment.

Another ineradicable habit of his (common to many tycoons) was to ring people up early in the morning. (He was usually in bed early himself.) I hated these dawn calls. He rang me once at 6.30 a.m., about nothing urgent. 'Allen,' I said, 'I never surface before nine,' and I hung up. It never happened to me again.

His relationship with women used to interest me a good deal. He liked their company, but usually as no more than a diversion, and he was inclined to be discomfited when he discovered that an attractive companion preferred real conversation to airy nothings. But although he sought relaxation with women he was far from adroit in his endeavours to establish an easy and amusing relationship with a cocktail companion or a lively dinner neighbour. He was no good at banter, either; he couldn't for the life of him chat a woman up. I think he really preferred the female to the feminine, and it was not difficult for an intelligent and sophisticated woman to get his measure. For some years before the war he and his brothers ran a bachelor establishment in Paddington, a Bohemian pad where heavy parties were frequent. I remember one which went on for three days, during which more or less the same crowd came and went—and came back for more.

Coping with a Crisis

I have never known anyone 'get away with murder' as Allen did—in an immense variety of situations. When some crisis had arisen in the firm's affairs he would think nothing of going off on a trip to America or Australia, leaving no directives, or even advice, for his senior colleagues and blandly assuming they would sort things out by the time he was back. It was a severe ordeal for those who were left to unravel the tangle, but more often than not they succeeded, though the credit they got could be less than casual.

He was never very orthodox at a staff conference of any kind. He would play ducks and drakes with an agenda, confuse the issues and often leave before the meeting came to an end. I used to think that he deliberately encouraged chaos at such meetings, partly because he bored easily, partly because he believed that if he stirred people up until feelings ran high it was likely that, in sheer desperation, they would hit upon a solution of whatever dilemma confronted them. I have seen him stoke up such situations over and over again, and very often with dramatic success. To see him deliberately provoke a disorderly discussion was an unexpected spectacle, but that anarchic atmosphere seemed to suit his temperament, and I can testify that from these eruptions the right solution often emerged.

Desperate Decisions

Allen's usual demeanour was easy and self-confident. But that expression of assurance concealed a highly strung nature which disclosed itself in several ways.

It was a tension, for example, which sometimes propelled him into precipitate and even desperate decisions, either about people or about problems. This led to instability in the upper levels of management: you could be top dog one day—and in the dog-house the next. When he had made up his mind, sometimes hastily, to sack someone on the staff, he often flinched from breaking the news himself and delegated a senior colleague to fire the victim. This habit was not due to any feelings of delicacy but wholly and visibly due to a lack of moral fibre. He was liable to bolt in a tight corner. Early in the war he contracted to buy a large quantity of black-market paper. A senior member of the staff remonstrated with him. 'All right,' said Allen, without a blush; 'you get out of it for me'—and went away for a week. This practice of involving others as scapegoats for his own lapses was attributable not only to moral cowardice but also to a decided streak of sadism in his nature. Those who lack what the Italians call the *dono di coraggio* often seem to camouflage this weakness by acts of calculated cruelty.

His reluctance to tell a man to his face that he was fired sometimes led to grotesque solutions. On one visit to Australia he decided to sack two of his staff there and to reprieve a third who had been at risk. But he avoided breaking the news, even at the airport when the three came to see him off. One of them, however, insisted 'You must tell us where we stand.' 'All right,' said Allen desperately—'*You* are out—*you* are out—*you* are in—and *I'm* off.' And off he went.

There were, too, occasions of another kind on which his nerve was liable to crack. When he was running The Bodley Head he was involved in a libel action about a book called *The Whispering Gallery*, which purported to be the memoirs of a diplomat. As a witness for the defence Allen was cross-examined by the formidable figure, Sir Patrick Hastings, and severely roughed-up in the process. Years afterwards he shuddered at the memory of the ordeal, and when the *Lady Chatterley* case came to court he was manifestly ill at ease and, indeed, declined to face the fast bowling as an opening bat and went in much lower down.

There were other instances, often trivial, when the same liability overcame him. The time, for example, when he gave some companions a lift in his Mercedes to the Book Fair at Florence. Coming over the Mont Cenis Pass he lost confidence in his gears and brakes, but managed to get down all right. The damage was done: he refused to drive further and took himself back to England, leaving his companions to find their own way to Florence. The man sent later to retrieve the Mercedes found nothing wrong with it.

The tensions in his temperament had another kind of consequence. He was liable to act too soon or too late, to plunge or to hesitate. He was irresolute. He could shelve a decision which his advisers considered urgent, or he could jump the gun. He found it difficult to rationalize a problem. One sad example of this disability arose over the Allen Lane Foundation, a

charitable trust which he set up in 1965 with a substantial endowment. As his wealth increased he was
urged by some of his closest friends to make further
provision in his lifetime, before his gifts became liable
to Estate Duty. He used to say he was easily able to
put another half-million or so into the Foundation,
and he was always 'going to see to it'. But he deferred
action until ten months before his death, and so the
additional £521,000 was eroded by Estate Duty to a
mere £70,000. He was equally dilatory, too, about
some of his family trusts. No rich man was ever so
badly caught in this as he was, and not through any
lack of counsel by his professional advisers.

The Stag at Bay

I rarely saw him lose his temper. His usual way of
expressing displeasure, either with a colleague or
friend, was to sulk. All the same there were occasions,
especially in the firm's most tempestuous two years,
1966 and 1967, when he had no alternative to having
it out with someone with whom he was at odds. I was
a spectator at some of these confrontations and
watched him, so to speak, behaving like a stag at bay.
His lips would shut more tightly than ever, his head
settle more deeply into his neck, and as the show-
down developed he reminded me of Sheridan's
choleric Sir Anthony Absolute—'an unforgiving eye
and a damn'd disinheriting countenance'.

The contradictions in Allen's behaviour were

perplexing. He could be wilful and ungenerous, and often was; but he was also capable of considerable compassion to people in his circle who were in some kind of distress. These acts of kindness were always imaginative and undemonstrative, and any expression of gratitude most genuinely embarrassed him.

Allen never played any part in public life. For one thing he did not feel strongly about any cause or problem. Nor was he inclined to give time to the inevitable meetings which such interests involve. He was not a committee man and he had neither the aptitude nor the patience for round-table discussions. Once or twice he was cajoled into becoming a governor of an educational body, but he displayed little interest in the policies and management of such institutions. He had no interest in politics, though he voted Labour, and he was equally indifferent to religion.

A Dedicated Farmer

For more than twenty-five years Allen developed a keen and sustained interest in farming. It is not un- common for businessmen, as they get richer, to acquire a farm as a prestige background and a source of tax rebate. To genuine countrymen these investors are 'clean-boot farmers', but Allen was not in this category. He came of country stock, farming was in his ancestral blood, and he had a real love for growing things. In 1942 he and his brother John (then in the RNVR) went to a farm sale at Reading. They had lunch in style, beforehand, at the celebrated Hind's Head at Bray and, according to Allen, John was sleepy at the sale and kept nodding—and that was the reason, Allen used to say, why the auctioneer knocked down the farm to them! It is typical that when they bought the farm they had no money to pay for it, but Allen went next day and raised the money from Martin's Bank.

He knew little about farming, and he was always frank about his early mistakes, most of which were due to over-staffing and insufficient managerial control. He believed that his farm should pay its way. It took time and hard work to get the run-down farm into good condition but in a few years its productivity per acre was exemplary, not least because Allen installed a system of irrigation and made other improvements which farmers working for a living cannot always afford.

In farming Allen followed the practice which he had found so beneficial in publishing—he diligently consulted people who had farming knowledge and experience. He often asked them down for a friendly hospitable lunch followed by a vigilant walk round his fields and buildings. He asked sensible questions and so received valuable answers. He revealed again his remarkable ability to involve others in his problems and to persuade them that he was genuinely wishing to learn.

Restoring Priory Farm, near Reading, to fertility whetted his appetite and fortified his confidence, and he went on to buy a bigger property, Chapmansford in north Hampshire. It was to be a corn and stock-rearing unit, run in conjunction with Priory Farm and under the same management: taking over, for example, young dairy stock not required for replacements in the milking herd. He followed the advice of his consultants (as he did in publishing) and drew a nice balance between logical modernizing and retaining the amenities of the traditional old buildings. He spent a lot of money on the corn-drying plant and on reclamation of the water-meadows: his concern was to bring the land up to its maximum productivity without impoverishing the soil.

He was too good a businessman not to appreciate the advantages of investing in land, but that was decidedly not his first consideration. He got fun from it, the same satisfaction as he did from publishing—the achievement of excellence. Had he been concerned in gaining the prestige of a squire, he would have left managers to run things the easy way, but his own control was always apparent, and he left both his farms in a condition any farmer would be proud of.

From what he used to tell me I always felt that Allen got from farming certain satisfactions which even publishing could not provide—a less hectic environment, for instance, more foreseeable results and a visual pleasure in the physical growth of crops and herds. In farming, too, he was not beset by the tensions which seem to be inseparable from dealing with large numbers of people. He fulfilled a good deal of his nature in farming, and perhaps from farming, too, he drew most of his happiness, especially in the last few years of his life. He needed it, for in those years he was desperately concerned with a crucial problem in Penguin affairs.

Problems of the Succession

For thirty years he had been the Supremo at Penguin's. Despite his unorthodox notions of management, and despite many hasty and wrong decisions, he had been, and had been seen to be, the boss. He had built the firm, seen it through many dicey phases, and given it international renown. And then, inevitably, he became preoccupied with the succession, as successful dictators are inclined—and indeed obliged —to be. There were two problems to be faced. The first was to give the Penguin enterprise an infrastructure which would protect it from the risk of a takeover after his death. The second was to find the man to replace him as leader. My account of the first of these problems will be more in place in the second part of this book where I consider landmarks in Penguin's development. In his later years it was the quest for a successor which occupied and distracted Allen even more than setting up a constitution to preserve Penguin's freedom and independence. He reluctantly retired as Managing Director in 1970, a few months before his death, but he kept on as Chairman until the end.

In the search for an heir he became feverish at times. Promising candidates were brought into the firm and subjected to a harassing scrutiny which hardly encouraged them to display or develop their capacities. In his anxiety Allen began to nourish suspicions about the motives of some of them, in a manner sometimes reminiscent of an Oriental potentate keeping a beady eye on aspirants to the Caliphate. (And in some cases his wariness was vindicated.) The home-bred birds usually turned out to be geese, not swans.

Another gambit, in these unhappy and distressing years, was to look outside publishing altogether for his successor and to canvass such people as a Cabinet minister, a distinguished barrister, two editors of national papers, a University Vice-Chancellor and the director of a famous College of Art. In these hectic reconnaissances Allen displayed once more his habitual inclination to make snap judgements. He would not take the time to determine the qualifications and attributes needed in the man to succeed him, and the method he was inclined to adopt was about as appropriate as picking the winner out of a hat. Even two months before his death he invited yet another distinguished man from outside the world of publishing to visit him. Over a bottle of champagne Allen pressed his visitor, then aged sixty, to join him as second-in-command for a year or two and then to mount the throne. The man was astonished at the suggestion which was, indeed, quite crazy, and even a second bottle made no difference. The truth, I suppose, is that although he knew he needed a strong right arm, he never really wanted to entrust Penguin's to anyone. I can see his point.

A Potent Personality

Within the thirty-five years during which Allen directed and dominated Penguin's he achieved the most potent influence in the history of British publishing. It was an adventurous and exhilarating feat, and it was often a hazardous one. Others, indeed, shared in the fulfilment of the enterprise, and the gods on the whole were benevolent. But it was incontestably Allen's creation and it bears the unique hallmark of his talent and temperament. To work with him one had to share his faith, accept his inspiration —and forgive him his trespasses. Many who went on the adventure failed to survive, and those who did all have scars to show for it. I have no illusions about the maestro; he could be, as one of his cronies affectionately called him, 'a right bastard'. Indeed he could, but my own memory of him, which is not likely to fade, is of an infuriating, mercurial comrade who was dearer to me than any other man in my life.

Sir Allen Lane. A portrait by Bryan Kneale, 1960.

Allen Lane as a young man in his mid-thirties.

II

LANDMARKS
AND MILESTONES

II

LANDMARKS AND MILESTONES

This book is not a biography of Allen Lane, nor is it a
history of Penguin Books. But there were landmarks
and milestones in Allen's life and the firm's growth
which seem to me to explain, or at least to illustrate,
the motives which governed his actions and behaviour.
Some of these landmarks are necessarily related to
Penguin policies, but I mention them in this memoir
only when they reveal Allen's approach to the problems which confronted him in his management of the
business.

Allen's life as a publisher lasted more than fifty
years. It began on St George's Day, April 23rd, 1919,
in his seventeenth year. A week before he went to work
at The Bodley Head, in Vigo Street, his surname had
been changed by deed-poll from Williams to Lane,
and at the same time his parents, two brothers and a
sister all took the new surname. This was done at the
request of the veteran publisher and Chairman of The
Bodley Head, John Lane. He was a distant relative of
Allen's mother, and when she asked him to take her
eldest son into the firm he readily agreed on condition
that Allen adopted the name of Lane. He had no
children, and he did not want his family name to
become extinct. Allen's mother, a strong character,
sensibly decided that it would be incongruous for
Allen alone to adopt her kinsman's name, so the

whole family changed from Williams to Lane. One of Allen's christian names was already Lane, so the young apprentice was now Allen Lane Williams Lane. He never used the full name, of course, nor even the initials. From 1919 he was always simply Allen Lane.

Born in Bristol

He was born in Bristol on September 21st, 1902, and brought up in a suburb of the city. His father was an architect of modest merit who worked in the municipal valuer's department; his mother came from a long line of yeoman farmers. The family spent their holidays at the farms of various relatives, and in his boyhood Allen developed an exuberant interest in all aspects of country activity. It survived throughout his life and, in his later years particularly, he spent his happiest times on his own farms. His father, a pleasant ruddy little man, devoted most of his leisure to manufacturing vegetable wines for the household, and in every room there were fermenting bowls of parsnip, cowslip, dandelion and many other home-made vintages. He used to brew cider, too, and had a local reputation as a connoisseur of cheddar cheese. Allen's mother was manifestly the head of the house: a genial farmer's-wife type of character with a mop of curly hair twice as big as Jennie Lee's. They were a close-knit and contented family, and were always to remain so.

It was during the First World War that young Allen

showed the first signs of a native cunning which he subsequently often displayed in his business life. I referred on page 19 to Allen's relish for *The Adventures of Tom Sawyer* and his special liking for the episode of whitewashing the fence. It is Allen's brother, Dick, who recalls the following parallel. The Lane children had been set to work to dig an allotment for growing vegetables. After ten minutes' toil with the spade Allen decided there was an easier way to get the job done. He let it be known among the young members of the church choir that free sweets would be issued on the Lanes' allotment next Saturday morning in return for a little agreeable work. There was a good response to his invitation and, supplied with forks, spades and an abundance of 'gob-stoppers', the volunteers soon had the plot ready for planting.

Of Allen's education at Bristol Grammar School nothing significant has been recorded. He appears to have been an average pupil who showed no particular aptitude for anything and was remembered by one of his form-masters as being below standard in Arithmetic and English. He remained so all his life. His letters, whether dictated or written in his own hand, were devoid of any distinction: they were pedestrian, often awkward and never felicitous. And adding up a column of figures was a slow and laborious exercise.

The Industrious Apprentice

He was five months short of his seventeenth birthday when he went to work for John Lane at The Bodley

Head. Uncle John, as Allen called him, had been publishing for thirty years when the young apprentice joined him. He had secured both renown and notoriety for The Bodley Head, and had many famous authors of the nineties on his list—Edmund Gosse, Ernest Dowson, Max Beerbohm, Aubrey Beardsley, Oscar Wilde, H. G. Wells, Arnold Bennett, Frederick Rolfe, and Anatole France (in translation). John Lane also published all the work of W. J. Locke, Agatha Christie's first six books and the first thirteen books of C. S. Forester. His list included a number of items which shocked a section of the public, and evoked severe criticism, such as the audacious *Yellow Book*. It was a censorious clergyman who wrote one of the pithiest comments on John Lane's list—

> Would there were more of the godly heart
> And less of the Bodley Head!

By the time Allen joined the firm its best days were over, and John Lane, at sixty-five, was getting bored with the business. He found Allen a useful dogsbody, willing to run his errands and cope with the usual chores. For his part Allen was keen and industrious, and soon took the opportunity to learn the rudiments of the trade. He began as a 'looker-out'—the chap who gathers the books together to fill an order. He also served as a packer and graduated to the job of delivering orders to the bookshops—by horse and cart—before becoming a traveller for the firm in London. He was ready to turn his hand to anything and he quickly picked up the basic principles of marketing books. It was during this industrious apprenticeship, too, that he first came to realize the meaning of quality in publishing. John Lane was fastidious about the printing and format of his books, and it was in these years that Allen, too, began to cultivate a concern for the visual values of publishing.

After a time Allen went to live with John Lane and his American wife at Lancaster Gate, and here he began to cultivate a social life. He was attractive, vivacious and available, and Uncle John's circle provided him with ample social opportunities. One friend he made at this time was Ben Travers, who had worked at The Bodley Head before the First World War and was later the successful playwright who created the popular Aldwych farces. John Lane asked Ben Travers and his wife to keep an eye on the ebullient Allen and to safeguard him from the seductive attractions of London life. 'But within a week', Ben Travers has recalled, 'it was he who was looking after us.' His work at The Bodley Head gave Allen opportunities to meet several writers of the day—tea with Thomas Hardy at Dorchester, where he also met John Drinkwater. The star Bodley Head author at this time was W. J. Locke, the popular romantic novelist, who asked Allen to stay with him at his villa in the south of France. What apparently impressed Allen most was that the villa had seven bathrooms. After a lecture by Bernard Shaw Allen asked him for his autograph. While signing the book the sage remarked, 'Young man, don't waste your time in collecting autographs. Use it instead in making your own autograph worth collecting.'

Trouble at The Bodley Head

By the time Uncle John died in 1925, The Bodley Head was in real trouble. Allen, now twenty-three, became a member of the board, and Chairman in 1930, and soon found himself at odds with his colleagues. One clash occurred when Allen wanted The Bodley Head to publish a book of Peter Arno's lively cartoons, *Peter Arno's Parade*, edited by Ben Travers. The rest of the board demurred. Allen at once said he would publish it under his own name. The board flinched from this one and then offered to publish the book but at Allen's personal risk. The book was a distinct success and was the first example of the flair which John Lane had also revealed in his palmiest days.

Allen's association with The Bodley Head was now nearing the end. After John Lane's wife's death in 1928 the Lane money all came to Allen, his two brothers and his sister, and Allen began to feel confident of his ability to set off on his own. He had become eager to try his luck with a cheap paperback series, but again his colleagues at The Bodley Head flinched from the proposal, and finally compromised by saying they would undertake distribution of the series—but again at his own risk. The Penguin adventure was about to begin, and the first ten volumes appeared on July 30th, 1935. In 1936 The Bodley Head went into voluntary liquidation—and Allen was launched. Although The Bodley Head was bearing no risk its name appeared on the covers of the first eighty titles. There is, indeed, some uncertainty about the early financing of the Penguin operation and about the responsibilities of the two firms. In the confusion about The Bodley Head's bankruptcy several printers appear not to have been paid for the Penguins they printed, but to these unfortunates Allen showed consideration and generosity when Penguin's got going. Only a few weeks before the bankruptcy The Bodley Head under Allen's persuasion had published a luxury edition of James Joyce's *Ulysses*. It has been a best-seller ever since and, indeed, has earned more than enough to cover The Bodley Head's deficiency at the time of its bankruptcy. When the assets of The Bodley Head were put up for sale in 1937, Allen made a bid but failed to acquire the firm, yet before the end of his life he was to have a new business of his own in The Bodley Head's old home in Vigo Street.

Allen was never quite sure when and where the notion of starting a cheap paperback series came into his head. John Lane, in fact, had experimented in this field as far back as 1909. He had published a translation of a book by a German officer, Lieutenant Bilse, called *Life in a Garrison Town*. It achieved great notoriety in Germany, and was eventually suppressed and its author court-martialled and imprisoned. After printing several editions of the book John Lane finally issued it, with a full-colour cover, at one shilling and three pence. Another reprint venture of The Bodley Head was an edition of its translations of Anatole France at half-a-crown, in orange cloth boards. There had been other pioneers in publishing cheap reprints. When W. H. Smith opened their first railway book-stall in 1848 there were several such series on display —the Railway Library, the Travellers' Library, the Run and Read Library. They were mostly novels of varying merit, ranging downward in price from one-and-sixpence to sixpence, and they all had an un-distinguished appearance. But before the century was out a better reprint product was becoming available, and of these the ones which deserved to survive— and, indeed, have done to this day—were the World's Classics and the Everyman Library, but both at a higher price than Penguins, and of course not paper-backs.

The Concept of Penguins

How far it was Allen's intention to improve on these pioneering ventures it is impossible to say. His own explanation was that it all began sometime in 1934 when he was returning from a weekend in the country with Agatha Christie. While he waited for his train he searched the bookstall for something to read on the journey, but found nothing except expensive titles and garish reprints of rubbish. Surely, he thought (or so he used to say) there should be a demand for good, well-produced literature at a modest price.

In the next few months he and his brothers, Dick and John, mulled over the decisions to be made—about authors, titles, format and finance. When they began to canvass opinion about the venture they met with a mixed reception. The Old Guard of publishing were sceptical and unsympathetic. Before Penguin's had really got going Allen was invited to justify his belief that such a paperback series could be viable. He was asked to address the Double Crown Club, a select company of publishers, printers, artists and book-collectors. Allen spoke his piece and was set upon. One of the opposition was Harold Raymond, then Chairman of Chatto and Windus, and one of the most respected figures in the business. Other senior publishers joined in denigrating the enterprise. It could not possibly succeed because not enough people would want a wretched paper-bound book. To sell at sixpence it would inevitably be a shoddy job. And if it did succeed (said others) it would ruin the book trade, and the publishing of serious literature would go to pieces.

There were others, younger ones, at the Double Crown dinner who got up and defended Allen, and he himself made confident rejoinders to some of the critics. So unabashed was he, indeed, that one senior member muttered to his neighbour, 'Cocky little sparrow, that chap!'

It was undeniably true at that time that many of the

best booksellers were reluctant to stock paperbacks for fear that the public, once they found that they could buy good reading for sixpence, would not be willing to pay the standard price for a novel, which in those days was seven-and-sixpence. There was a feeling too, not wholly unjustified, that the cheap competitor might contaminate orthodox publishing.

There were other objections. By 1935 books had become so accessible through municipal and circulating libraries that the incentive of individual book-collecting had diminished. Paperbacks were rapidly perishable and difficult to display. Even if these predictions were not fulfilled, the critics continued, the publishers would not be such fools as to let Penguin's under-cut the hardcover sales of successful titles. And, finally, Penguin's, a firm launched with a nominal capital of £100, would be unable to withstand a long financial siege if things went less than well. One cynical commentator on the project was Jonathan Cape, a most shrewd and successful publisher. 'If Lane wants paperback rights of some of my titles why shouldn't I take his money off him? I know he'll fail!'

Whether or not these doubts had substance Penguin's got off to a sticky start. Allen was not discouraged by the poor flow of early orders and, characteristically, pitched in himself. He went to see the head buyer of Woolworth's and managed to get from him an initial order of 10,000 copies of each of the first ten Penguin titles. A further order from

Woolworth's within a week convinced Allen that this example would persuade other booksellers to follow suit—as indeed they did. Within a few months it was clear that the Penguin was on its feet.

The First Ten

The first ten titles published in July 1935 were a safe and unsurprising choice. There were a couple of choice detective thrillers, one by Agatha Christie and one by Dorothy L. Sayers. There was *Gone to Earth* by Mary Webb, a trivial but very successful writer who had been excessively eulogized by Stanley Baldwin, the most ardent country-loving Prime Minister Britain had ever had. There were Beverley Nichols's amiable excursion into autobiography, *Twenty-five*; the evergreen *William* by E. H. Young; Compton Mackenzie's *Carnival*; Eric Linklater's *Poet's Pub*; and *Madame Claire* by Susan Ertz. The first batch of ten was completed by two distinctively superior titles —Hemingway's vivid war novel, *A Farewell to Arms*, and *Ariel*, the felicitous life of Shelley by André Maurois. Press notices were scanty and cool. *The Times Literary Supplement* of July 25th, 1935, saw no future at all for sixpenny paperbacks and wrote them off in a curt footnote, and two years later, when the Pelicans began, there was no editorial mention of them in the *T.L.S.*

These first ten Penguins were a sensible choice for a start. They were books which had done well in hard covers, and at sixpence instead of seven-and-sixpence they were a pretty obvious bargain. During the next eighteen months the list grew steadily on much the same principles of choice, and in each batch there were two or three titles of exceptional distinction: *South Wind* by Norman Douglas, *A Passage to India* by E. M. Forster, *Crome Yellow* by Aldous Huxley, *The Purple Land* by W. H. Hudson and equally prestigious titles by Conrad, Evelyn Waugh and T. F. Powys. During this initial period the Penguin policy was plainly demonstrated: it was to be a library of cheap reprints, complete and unabridged, mainly of fiction but also, to a lesser extent, of biography, travel and *belles lettres*.

Business was so brisk in the first few months as to tax the distributive resources of The Bodley Head beyond their capacity, and Penguin's had now to make its own arrangements.

Days in the Crypt

The young firm took over the lease of a derelict crypt under Holy Trinity church in Euston Road. The rent was £200 a year, and there were no rates. Around the walls of this desolate cellar were bricked-in coffins, each with its nameplate attached. There was no water, no sanitation, so a utensil was provided which the office boy took upstairs every night and tipped in the shabby churchyard. The girls on the staff were given sixpence a week each to pay for visits to the public lavatory at Great Portland Street Station. As this Black Hole of the Crypt was below ground it was cool in summer but perishing cold in the winter.

Working in this cramped crypt was arduous and inconvenient. But it had lighter moments. Loud noises were carried upstairs by the ventilation grille to the church above, and caution had to be particularly observed when a service was in progress. There were inevitably 'incidents', as when a packer hit his thumb with a mallet and bellowed an oath just when the parson conducting a wedding upstairs had put the question, 'Wilt thou take this woman to be thy wife?' After a few months the firm acquired a small suite of offices in Great Portland Street and the crypt became the warehouse. In 1937 the whole firm moved out to a new building on the Bath Road at Harmondsworth, fifteen miles from Charing Cross, and it has been there ever since. But the site of three and a half acres was soon too small for the rapidly expanding business, and with the new buildings added since 1937 Penguin Books now cover about four times the acreage of the original building. Most of this considerable space consists of warehousing for the many millions of books always in stock of the massive list maintained of Penguins and all the other series.

From Reprints to Originals

During Penguin's first year it began to consolidate itself as a reprint series of quality books, and at that stage Allen had not foreseen that it was capable of developments in new directions. What happened next —and was to happen many times in the following years—was one of Allen's encounters with new acquaintances whom he promptly and avidly questioned about his firm's activities and prospects. I was one of them. I was introduced to Allen by Krishna Menon, an Indian barrister domiciled in London and a devoted fighter for Indian independence. There were at that time ten arduous years ahead of him before his dream was fulfilled in 1947. He was a man of great zeal and tenacity, and not the easiest person to get on with. Freedom-fighters seldom are.

Most of my working life up to that time had been in adult education. I was editing *The Highway*, the monthly magazine of the Workers' Educational Association, and was a busy member of the WEA National Executive, among whose members were R. H. Tawney, J. J. Mallon, A. D. Lindsay (Master of Balliol), Archbishop Temple, Arthur Creech Jones and many other Labour leaders of the 'thirties. Our youngest colleague was Richard Crossman, then an ebullient and voluble Oxford don of considerable force and *panache*. For some years I had also been a Staff Tutor in English Literature for the London University Extra-Mural Board, which I left in 1934 to become Secretary of the British Institute of Adult Education, a lively research body and pressure group, devoted to the enlargement of opportunities of further education for adult workers. The emergence of Pen-

Allen Lane holding the Gold Medal bestowed on him by the Royal Society of Arts. With him is W. E. Williams.

The first Penguin office and warehouse: the crypt of Holy Trinity church, Portland Place.

guin's seemed to me a heaven-sent opportunity for making it an ally and collaborator in the mission in which I was so deeply involved. It is material to say how this evangelistic fervour came to possess me. I had been trained to be a Minister in the Congregational Church, and was on the brink of being ordained, at a tender age, when I found myself doubting the doctrines I was required to accept, despite the fact that they were more liberal than those of any other Christian denomination. I defected to education, I suppose, because in that field I could find scope for my deep social concern and idealistic beliefs.

The Pelicans Appear

So when I first met Allen I suggested that Penguin's might join the current cultural crusade by starting a parallel series of cheap books on a wide range of intellectual interests—philosophy, psychology, history, literature, science. He responded immediately and enthusiastically, and off I went to put the idea on paper. At this stage, a colleague of mine joined in. He was H. L. Beales, then a Reader in History at the London School of Economics, and as deeply involved as I was in adult education.

The books in the new series were to be called Pelicans, and the small editorial board to select them consisted of Krishna Menon, myself, Beales and Sir Peter Chalmers-Mitchell, who had been Secretary of the Zoological Society. The first Pelican to be published, in May, 1937, made Penguin history. It was

Shaw's *Intelligent Woman's Guide to Socialism and Capitalism* for which the author supplied a whole new section on Sovietism and Fascism. This new material was the first original creative publishing to appear under the firm's imprint, an innovation which was soon to be considerably expanded. The Pelicans, like the Penguins, were priced at sixpence. The first group were all reprints of authoritative titles by Halévy, Roger Fry, Clive Bell, Fabre, Freud, Jeans and Julian Huxley, but these reprints were to be followed shortly by specially commissioned new books on philosophy, English literature, ballet, architecture, human physiology, archaeology and ornithology. As the years went by, new Pelican originals, as distinct from reprints, became the rule rather than the exception, and, apart from single volumes, whole series of new titles, specially written as Pelicans, were built up in such subjects as history, philosophy, psychology, English literature and so on.

Within a short time the original editorial board broke up, in 1939, partly through differences of opinion and partly by Allen's caprice. Chalmers-Mitchell died, Krishna Menon and Beales dropped out. Henceforth the choice of titles was left mainly to me, ably assisted by Eunice Frost who had a wide and perceptive knowledge of books. She had come into Penguin's as Allen's secretary and Man Friday, and the further she went up the ladder the greater contribution she made. She was to become a powerful influence on Penguin policy.

When the first Pelicans were published the intention behind them was to provide the serious general reader with definitive books on a wide range of intellectual interests, a purpose similar to the one which was later to be implicit in the famous Third Programme of BBC radio. There was initially no implicit design of building a library of modern knowledge at a modest cost. But Pelicans, in fact, became such a library, and, what is more, a library serving not only the general reader of serious purpose but also the great body of students pursuing courses in the universities and other institutions of higher education. This provision of books which proved to be ancillaries to educational prospectuses was to have an obvious value to the growth of the firm, for it has ensured a steady demand in bulk for these titles year after year. It has thus provided what might have been a speculative, if worthy, enterprise with a reliable and considerable economic backbone of revenue. For more than thirty-five years Pelicans have been the basis of a vertebrate structure of creative original publishing which came to include many other similar species such as King Penguins, Penguin Specials, Penguin Classics, Penguin Modern Painters, Puffins and the Pelican History of Art—as well as numerous other series in the vast Penguin list. A major development in this tradition occurred in 1964 when Penguin Educational was set up and was an immediate success.

The preparatory work on Penguin Educational was done by Christopher Dolley, who is now Chairman and Managing Director of Penguin's. But when he took over the American company in 1966 the development of the new series was entrusted to Charles Clark, one of the most able editors the firm has ever had, and one of the three editors who have left Penguin's since Dolley took over. Charles Clark ensured that Penguin Educational would revolutionize the rapidly expanding market for text-books at all levels, from the primary school to the university, and this thriving and lively enterprise has become a field of major growth and another brilliant manifestation of the educational motive which Pelicans first demonstrated nearly forty years ago.

The Decisive Event

The bold step of launching Pelicans seems to me the most decisive in the firm's history. It could never have attained the summits of its present reputation and value if it had remained a reprint operation and had failed to avow and reveal a specific educational purpose; and it could not have attained the economic stability it has enjoyed for over thirty-five years without the considerable monetary contribution made by the success of Pelican originals and the other related series I have mentioned on the preceding page. In its earlier years Penguin's built up a massive collection of the best fiction in the language and had no competitors in this field. But that rich vein was bound to become exhausted, and nowadays the fiction

list has to rely not on the Old Guard of Wells, Lawrence, Conrad, Galsworthy, Arnold Bennett and
Priestley, but on more recent fiction of more modest
merit. There are now no ten-title batches of one
author. Fiction is now the back runner in the vast and
varied list.

When Allen first asked me to justify the policy
which put such an emphasis on 'serious' books I was
able to put him in the picture about the widespread
growth of adult education which was taking place in
the 'thirties. This was not only true about the growth
of the WEA and formal classes in adult education
but was equally significant in the growth of such semi-
educational bodies as the Women's Institutes and the
Townswomen's Guilds. There was other evidence,
too, building up of a new interest in the arts. In 1935
I had launched through the British Institute of Adult
Education a plan called 'Art for the People'. The basis
of this was to assemble loan-exhibitions from well-
disposed private owners and circulate them among
small towns and villages where original works of art
were never seen. It caught on and developed rapidly.
In 1940, indeed, it was selected as the pattern for the
Government's creation of CEMA, the Council for the
Encouragement of Music and the Arts, later to become the Arts Council.

It was in the 'thirties, too, that the BBC, responding
to the influence of John Reith, was making its influence felt through radio. It was encouraging the wide
discussion of public affairs and, at the same time,

diligently cultivating knowledge and interest in the arts, the social sciences and international problems. It had an audience of millions for its serious programmes no less than for its recreational ones.

There were other elements in the climate of the 'thirties. The depression had stimulated social concern, and the political landscape was ominous enough to encourage public interest in international affairs. The lost battles of Republican Spain, and the threatening posture of Hitler and Mussolini, were sinister portents. The 'thirties were a period of foreboding, and both press and radio confirmed the widespread public concern. In short it was a time of taking serious thought about our values and arming our minds for confronting social and political hazards. It was, indeed, just the time for beginning so purposeful a series as Pelicans.

The Penguin Specials

This conviction was ratified by another series of originals which began to appear soon after Pelicans had been launched. In the same year, 1937, the first Penguin Specials were published and these, too, immediately established a landmark. By that time the cold war was hotting up, and the dictators were browbeating the free world. The Penguin response to these matters of intense public concern was to publish a new series of books urgently commissioned from experts in current international affairs. The titles of these books reveal their topicality—*Searchlight on Spain, Blackmail or War?, Europe and the Czechs, Mussolini's Roman Empire, Germany Puts the Clock Back, The Jewish Problem, What Hitler Wants, Poland*. Not all the Specials were about the approaching storm: there were other urgent matters for discussion —such as *Britain's Health, British Agriculture, The Case for Family Allowances, World Shipping, The Kingship of Christ, Twentieth Century Socialism*.

The Specials caught on. Very many were best-sellers which clocked up sales of a quarter of a million in a few weeks. Indeed the massive sales of the Specials—and also the early Pelicans—produced a vital and unforeseen bonus when paper rationing was imposed as one of the essential wartime controls. The ration was based on current consumption, and because of the very large Penguin sales from 1935 to 1941 its quota was substantial enough not only to maintain all the existing series but also to launch several new ventures. During the war four of these were begun—the King Penguins, the firm's first books in colour; the Puffin Picture Books for children; the Puffin Story Books; and Penguin Modern Painters edited by Kenneth Clark. While the war was on, moreover, there was being planned a series which proved as popular and prestigious as the Pelicans and the Specials. This was the Penguin Classics, edited by the late E. V. Rieu, the first of which (his own transla-tion of *The Odyssey*) appeared in January of 1946.

The war years were a period of expansion for

Penguin's, and as soon as the opportunity for a new series appeared Allen gave full reign to his enthusiasm and boldness of decision. In the post-war years of further progress many other series were developed. The significant feature of most of them was that they were outside the field of fiction and outside the reprint category. They represented facets of Penguin as the Popular Educator, a rôle in which Allen took increasing pride. By 1956 less than half of the ten million Penguin titles sold in that year were reprints of fiction. The other half, the more-than-half, were new books designed in various ways to provide the public with the pleasures and discoveries of the mind. The ratio between fiction and education has increased year by year.

The Popular Educator

No one took more satisfaction in this enlargement of the original purpose of Penguin's than Allen himself and, capricious though he could be, he never wavered in his devotion to the concept of Penguin's as the Popular Educator. If Penguin's had remained a reprint organization devoted to the low-cost production of fiction it could never have become the dynamic educational influence which it is today. It is significant, too, that of the many paperback series which other publishers have issued the most reputable and, indeed, successful have been those which followed the Penguin example of going way out beyond the limited world of fiction. It is also worth noting that although hardback publishers were cynical—and often unco-operative—about the Penguin enterprise during its early years, they have become without exception not only willing to lease reprint rights to Penguin but also to follow its example of paperback originals. This, too, gave immense satisfaction to Allen: he felt that his mission had been abundantly fulfilled.

Allen was always at his best when a new project was under way. One notable venture in which he took a keen interest was the Puffins for children. First there was the series called Puffin Picture Books edited by Noel Carrington. This was followed by Puffin Story Books edited for many years by Eleanor Graham.

The Puffin innovation has been expanded in recent years by Kaye Webb, one of whose brainwaves was the Puffin Club started in 1967, which, on June 28th, 1972, enrolled its 100,000th member.

Once Allen cottoned on to a scheme he was very quick indeed at gauging its potential, and particularly good at coping with the practicalities involved in launching series like the Pelicans. Money had to be raised to finance the new operation, time-tables of meticulous accuracy had to be drawn up, booksellers had to be persuaded to make more room on their shelves for yet more paperback titles. To these essential tasks, and many similar ones, he brought his tireless energy and mastery of his trade. All his editors had to do was to secure the new titles and make sure that the writers they commissioned understood precisely the purpose of such a new series as Pelicans or

Specials or Puffins. He never interfered with them and they, in turn, were not harassed by the technicalities of publication.

When Pelicans were amply fulfilling the hopes we had of them Allen wrote me a characteristic letter.

27th April, 1943.

My dear Bill,

Your *Book of English Essays* in Pelican's is due to be published in July. It is no. 99 in the Pelican List, so we shall soon be celebrating the first Pelican century. This event calls for a party for those who have been involved in it, and when we meet next week we must discuss the details.

I can't tell you how much I rejoice in Pelican's Progress. When we began Penguin's in the summer of 1935 I hadn't a thought of producing anything but reprints of good quality. When you and I first discussed the Pelican idea my eyes were immediately opened to an exciting new possibility, and I could begin to visualize the expansion of the original idea in many ways. And it all began in that quiet little back-room of yours in 29, Tavistock Square.* Whoever could have expected such a publishing revolution to begin during these years of turmoil? I hope we'll have a lot more excitement before we're finished.

Yours,

Allen.

* The office of the British Institute of Adult Education.

That last sentence was certainly fulfilled. The original Penguin concept was developed in many other patterns, but it is not my business in this book to narrate the Penguin Story beyond its earlier formative years when I was so closely concerned with the choice of books published in Penguins, Penguin Specials, Penguin Poets and Pelicans. But I can testify that, during those years, the presence and personality of the founder were the decisive factors in the evolution of the firm. He was fortunate in finding and using many devoted men and women as his collaborators, but they were no less lucky in working with such a dynamic leader.

An Erratic Administrator

Allen was not a good administrator. The result was that, in some respects, Penguin affairs were sketchily handled. He never quite grasped, for example, the niceties of budgeting or the tidal mysteries of cash flow, and he never seemed able to hire good enough people to run the firm's finances; as a rule, indeed, they were so inarticulate that their interpretations were more oracular than intelligible. To resolve these problems Allen's solution, for many years, was to invoke the aid of the Bank, which was Martin's. Never was a man better served by his bank. Martin's were invariably paternal, or, at least, avuncular in their attitude and behaviour to this eager innovator, and this was significant in two ways. It shows how persuasive, how charming, Allen was; and it shows, too, how perceptive and how accurate Martin's were in their assessment of his flair and of the firm's inherent strength. He must have been one of the last to benefit from an element in banking which is on its way out as the mergers and take-overs eradicate the personal factor and leave decisions to the computer.

But the solidity and support Allen got from Martin's did not prevent him from seeking guidance on the firm's finances in other quarters. He was always taking his books and his balance-sheets to firms of City accountants, jumping on and off the merry-go-round of financial consultation. The trouble was that he didn't know enough about money matters to assess the advice he received, and also, because he was hasty and impatient, he switched too quickly from one adviser to another, not giving any of them enough time to diagnose his problems. Eventually the firm ran into serious financial difficulties which threatened to restrict its expansion in several necessary ways, and in 1966 and 1967 had to cope with a critical situation which shook Allen badly. The crisis was overcome by measures which had to include raising a large debenture, a step which Allen hated to take. Crises of this kind are, of course, liable to occur in a business expanding as rapidly as Penguin's was, but prudent and far-sighted administration at the top could have identified the danger signals and prevented a call to panic stations. Three senior executives were held responsible by Allen for this crisis and all three were relieved of their commands. After two anxious years matters were under control again, but the experience left its mark on Allen.

Editorial Policy

But his indifference to administrative procedures was, paradoxically, beneficial in some other sectors of the firm's affairs: above all, in editorial matters. One of the distinctive features of Penguin's has always been the high quality and wide reputation of its numerous series—Pelicans, King Penguins, the Penguin Classics, the Buildings of England, the Pelican History of Art, the Puffins, the Penguin Specials, the Handbooks and such magazines (no longer published) as *Science News*, *New Biology*, *Music Magazine*, *Film Review* and *Penguin New Writing*. None of these triumphs of publishing emerged from committee procedures or, indeed, from anything beyond the minimum routines of consultation. Every series had an editor with plenary powers. Initially each editor submitted his plan in broad terms, and discussed details about size, illustrations, production costs, printings, periodicity of publication and so on. At this stage Allen was always deeply involved and always very co-operative. Once these details were agreed each individual editor was left to get on with his series. He was not required to consult the High Command about anything unless he wished to, and was given an unqualified free hand. It was this freedom and consideration which made so many distinguished editors happy to serve the Penguin cause. This was why Allen was able to secure the

devoted and skilful services of such authorities as Sir
Nikolaus Pevsner, Noel Carrington, E. V. Rieu, John
Lehmann, Eleanor Graham, Edward Young, Sir Max
Mallowan, Kenneth Clark, Sir Alfred Ayer, Michael
Abercrombie, G. B. Harrison, Professor C. A. Mace,
Dr Gordon Jacob, Hubert Phillips, James Fisher and
so many others. He left them alone to pick titles and
writers for their particular series, and I cannot remember their choices ever being disputed. From time to
time he would take them out to lunch or dinner and
listen to how things were going in their domain. Some
years ago Allen commissioned Rodrigo Moynihan,
R.A., to paint a large picture called 'After the Conference'. It depicted nineteen of the editors standing
about at a cocktail party. There were indeed, from
time to time, parties of this kind, for us to meet each
other, but never were these agreeable social occasions
preceded or followed by anything as formal as a conference. That impressive painting hangs in the foyer
of the Penguin office where it no doubt suggests to
visitors that the editorial business of Penguin's is
formally conducted in the company's boardroom. The
editors were not even gathered together for Mr
Moynihan to paint them: we each 'sat' separately for
him, and in due course he assembled his sketches on
the large canvas.

An Editorial Quartet

The Penguin editorial methods in Allen's time and
mine were certainly informal, but there is nevertheless

no doubt that they were effective. They suited all concerned and, above all, they suited Allen. He hated paper-work, and he hated the protocol of orthodox office-meetings of any kind. In some ways he carried this dislike to excessive lengths, but in editorial matters informality yielded excellent dividends. I have made in an earlier paragraph a reference to the 'High Command'. I used the words ironically, as I shall now explain. Overall editorial decisions were taken by four of us—Allen, myself, Eunice Frost, and Alan Glover, who joined the firm in 1944. We considered the plans for every new series in a general way, but the major part of our commitment was the selection of all the Penguins and, after the first few years, all the Pelicans and the Penguin Specials. The High Command was in some ways a bizarre body, and it carried informality to the ultimate degree.

Alan Glover was a quite brilliant editor, especially of classical literature. He was widely read, in many disciplines and many languages; his knowledge was encyclopaedic in scale and precision; and among his technical skills was a speed and capacity for proof-reading which was a revelation even to experienced printers. Of Eunice Frost I have spoken before. Women of her calibre are not rare, but in her time they rarely reached a place of importance in a publisher's office. She certainly did. Beginning as Allen's secretary in the Portland Street crypt, she soon revealed qualities which were to make her one of the decisive personalities of the firm.

It was, then, a peculiar, almost implausible, quartet and yet for more than twenty years it was the editorial mainspring of Penguin Books. It worked, too, in ways which, even by Allen's standards, went the limit in unorthodoxy. To begin with, we met more often than not outside the Penguin office, partly because three of us lived in London and partly because Allen always welcomed the opportunity to get away from Harmondsworth. We did hold meetings sometimes at the Penguin office in Harmondsworth but more often we met at my office, and throughout my working life I have always been lucky enough to have a quiet and commodious office. In the first few years, then, we met at the British Institute of Adult Education in Tavistock Square. Then, when I went to the War Office in 1940 to create and direct the Army Bureau of Current Affairs (ABCA), it was in one of the Military Annexes, first Curzon Street House and then Eaton Square. And finally, when I became Secretary-General of the Arts Council we often met at its delightful old home in 4 St James's Square.

All of us except Allen had done a good deal of reading before we came to these meetings and there were always many books and typescripts on the table about which we made our comments and reached decisions. As he had not read the stuff, Allen's participation at this stage was limited, yet his interest in the proceedings was evident and he frequently came in with comments on our discussion which helped to clarify our opinions and criticisms. He was very much

An early Penguin. Early Pelicans.

John Lane's Vigo Street office, to which Allen Lane returned with his Penguin Press.

in the act and I was repeatedly struck by his instructive grasp of our principles of selection. From time to time we would invite a series editor to join us and outline his proposals for new titles.

Lunch at the Barcelona

After our London meetings we almost always lunched together, and for many years we did so week by week at a modest little Spanish restaurant in Beak Street, the *Barcelona*, run in those days by a genial gastronome called Carbonnel. Over these lunches we laid aside the business of discussing individual titles and settled down to the examination of major editorial principles. Fortified by innumerable *porrons* of sturdy wine from Carbonnel's family vineyard, we tackled major issues and often kept it up until 5 o'clock. I have never known more lively and penetrating sessions than those, and Allen's relish of the controversy that often developed was immense. Should we go in for picture covers? Should we begin doing five or ten at a time of the major modern novelists—Lawrence, Wells, Conrad, Aldous Huxley, Hemingway, Graham Greene, Priestley? (This we did, in fact, with immense success, but it was an innovation about which it took us a long time to decide.) Were we taking enough care with our 'blurbs'? What were the best ways to put our books across?—e.g. Penguin exhibitions? Penguin Weeks in bookshops? Literary luncheons? A house magazine? Selective advertising?

A Penguin Book Club? Or, again, were our Pelicans, Classics and other 'educational' series sufficiently available on college campuses? Were we publishing too many titles? Was our monthly publication list properly balanced? Should we start a series of Penguin Music Scores, Penguin Modern Painters, Penguin Poets? (And we did.)

The agenda for these lunchtime debates was inexhaustible, and very often controversial too. Eunice Frost and I were inclined to be vehement in our submissions; Glover was often cynical; and Allen enjoyed it all immensely. When feelings ran high and differences became acute he used, metaphorically, to rub his hands and, literally, call for more wine. When risks were involved he was almost always willing to take them, and the more adventurous a project seemed the more likely he was to adopt it.

For many years the sessions at the *Barcelona* were the crucible of Penguin policies. They were impromptu, uncompromising and untidy. Eunice Frost used to jot down the decisions but there were no minutes and no memoranda. It was not the way to run a business, I suppose, but it was in fact the foundation on which a successful business and an international reputation were established. It was also, of course, a basis of operations which was bound to change as the firm expanded, and change indeed it did—but only after twenty years or so.

Allen's nostalgia for those informal and incandescent sessions at the *Barcelona* never seemed to diminish, and when he was beset, in the last few years of his life, by the complex issues of big business he constantly compared them with the exciting challenges we had accepted and somehow resolved when the whole thing was a vivid and unpredictable adventure.

Between 1955 and 1965 the firm changed in many ways, as a growing concern is bound to do. Both Allen and I, while accepting the inevitable, did not like some of the changes and we both indulged sometimes in nostalgia for the good old days. On the eve of my retirement from the Penguin Board in 1965 Allen wrote to me from his villa in Spain.

El Fenix, Carvajal, Spain.
April 14th, 1965.

My dear Bill,

I find this an extremely difficult letter on which to get started, not because there's so little to say but *au contraire* there is so much, and lacking your lucidity I find it hard to marshal my thoughts. The only thing I can do is to let them tumble out, and I'll endeavour to set them down. I have been thinking about the old days when we used to meet every week at your office and then adjourn to the Barcelona for those exciting discussions about what we should do next. Although I was never conscious of following any deliberate policy, a pattern seemed to develop over the years. By judicious pruning, some cross-fertilization and the practice of good husbandry the growth was controlled until it became the plant which you this year, and I in two years, will hand over to the next generation to tend. It has taken almost exactly half my life, and most certainly the most rewarding part of it, and you know and I know exactly how much you have influenced both the enterprise and me over this period. I don't think that either of us could have visualized what it was going to become, but both of us having a good streak of idealism and a certain toughness of purpose have made it very much in our own image. What happens after our time is beyond our control. As good gardeners or farmers we can only do our best to see that the soil is kept in good heart, free of weeds, and that the crops are not forced but allowed a natural growth in the knowledge that if these principles are followed our successors will continue to have the satisfaction from it that we have had ourselves.

In conclusion what I have valued most has been the close friendship we have enjoyed over these many years, and I look forward to many more years of companionship when we can sit and drink and talk of life and love.

Yours,

Allen.

From time to time we invited one of the series editors to join us at these informal sessions. Sir

Nikolaus Pevsner, the King Penguin editor, recalls one of these occasions on which he got a memorable impression of how we sometimes behaved. He wanted us to do a book on the French archaeological excavations at Agarit. As we pushed the idea around, says Pevsner, I took a cynical view of his proposal and finally brought the argument to a crude conclusion by saying, 'Agarit, Agarit, oh bugger it!' A wide variety of moods used to prevail at our *Barcelona* sessions, but they certainly evolved the principles and values of the incomparable Penguin achievement in its first twenty years.

Penguin's Overseas

One of Allen's major contributions to Penguin's was his success in opening up foreign markets, and by 1955 over half of the annual output was being exported overseas. Long before then, too, he had established subsidiary companies in the U.S.A. and Australia. This expansion inevitably involved him in much trial and error, and never were his qualities of persistence and pertinacity more tested than in these complicated operations. Some of the difficulties were due, it must be said, to certain of his other characteristics, notably his impulsiveness and his inconsistency.

It was during these expansionist efforts that he developed the practice which was to grow on him of what I used to call 'flirting with the future'. He began to toy with the idea of joining forces with other powerful publishers. He appeared to have caught the bug of empire-building; but it became evident in the course of time that this was a hobby rather than anything else, an indulgent game which appealed to his peasant shrewdness.

A Bad Start in America

Before the war he had established an American subsidiary. It was, in effect, no more than an import agency, and it did quite well. Wartime difficulties hampered its growth, and when the war was over Allen set about building up a fully-fledged subsidiary. The endeavour was bedevilled from the start, mainly because of his method of instant government. He picked the wrong man to begin with, as he so often did. To mitigate the consequences he precipitately persuaded someone else to sort things out. This was a very able and versatile man, Victor Weybright, who had been one of Winant's clever attachés at the American Embassy in London. Allen fell for him completely, and even bestowed on him the accolade by naming Weybright as god-father to his third daughter. It proved an abortive alliance, mainly because Allen's suspicions were aroused by the discovery that Weybright, too, had imperial longings and was not willing to see Penguin Books Inc. become a vassal dependency. To my mind Weybright discharged his responsibilities admirably and, in particular, resisted the temptation to lower Penguin's to the paperback level which, at the time, prevailed in the American market. A breach was inevitable, and the resultant row was so violent that Allen never spoke to Weybright again, nor ever confided to me what his case against the man really was. As for Victor Weybright, he behaved with dignity when the calamity occurred, and although he knew that I had a certain influence on Allen, he never invoked my intercession. The rupture between them must have been seismic in its intensity.

Affairs in America took a decided turn for the better in 1949 when Harry Paroissien, who had joined Penguin's after the war, was sent out to Baltimore to make a fresh start. After a long experience of publishing in England he was able to make a good job of it in America, and under him both the prestige and the sales flourished. But it was not long before Allen began again to flirt with American publishers in plans for some kind of joint association. He always enjoyed these overtures, especially when the Americans, taking them more seriously than he did, used to make urgent flying visits to England to advance the negotiations. Allen always liked to have a simmering pot on the fire. He discussed co-operation with at least five major American publishers, always on the presumption that they would take over the American Penguin's and apply their know-how to expanding the enterprise. When eventually he found himself involved in such a partnership with Houghton Mifflin he began to regret it and did not rest until he bought back his independence from them. They had observed the terms of the treaty meticulously, but Allen's basic allergy to all alliances was bound to prevail. Once a pact was agreed he began to develop suspicions of a subtle plot to erode his power. When he finally decided to go it alone in America, Penguin Books Inc. began to give Allen his peace of mind again, although in later years the American company has had its share of crises.

The Australian Penguin Company, too, went through its vicissitudes for several years, mainly because of Allen's impatient decisions to replace its management from time to time. Finally it achieved some equilibrium when Allen's younger brother, Dick, took over in 1955, and it is now a flourishing partner in the Penguin Commonwealth. Allen made mistakes in trying to establish and consolidate the firm overseas, almost always because of hasty and impetuous decisions.

Allen as Ambassador

On the other hand he had gifts which had very positive and beneficial bearings upon the firm's development abroad. For example, he made frequent journeys to America and Australia on goodwill missions. Invariably, and unlike many of his British colleagues, he devoted a lot of time to visiting booksellers on these visits and enlightening them about Penguin methods and objectives. He was always a diligent and persuasive evangelist, and he well understood the virtues of the personal touch. He never concentrated his attention on the big retailers but applied it equally and tirelessly on the more modest booksellers. He knew the value of the grass-roots. One of Allen's contributions to Penguins was in the rôle of ambassador, not only in America and Australia but equally in Africa, India, and the West Indies, and the immense prestige (and turnover) the firm enjoys abroad is mainly attributable to his tireless ability to persuade the book trade everywhere to recognize the distinctive merits of Penguin policy and practice. A major Penguin growth field is overseas sales, and the boom is only beginning in an area which Allen so assiduously cultivated. His power of making effective personal contacts, especially at what are called the lower levels, was certainly one of Allen's most vital and effective attributes.

Flirting with the Future

In this country, as well as abroad, he was deeply engrossed in flirting with the future and discussing alliances with other publishers. As the firm expanded, especially from the mid-fifties, and grew from its modest and tentative beginnings into an empire, Allen began to show a genuine concern to explore the possibilities of consolidating what he had built up. There was also, despite his success, a nervous streak in Allen, and he evidently felt he should examine means of insuring against accidents to the firm.

He made overtures, or encouraged them, to several British publishers, and led some of them to believe that he was more interested than he really was in some kind of merger or partnership. The pattern of these discussions seldom varied. One of its usual features was that Allen would be seeming to pursue the negotiations purposefully and then would slow them down, so to speak, to a crawl and even suspend them for months at a time and re-open them later on. Some of these flirtations, indeed, lasted for years, and although the two parties were, so to speak, 'engaged' to be married sometime in the future (or 'walking out' as they say in the north), both of them came to realize that there would never be a wedding. But in one case the negotiations were developed so far that they seemed likely for some time to be agreed by all parties.

A University Trust

Allen had often said to me that he would like to see the firm taken into some kind of protective custody so that, after his death, it would be able to preserve its identity and safeguard the values and objects which it had developed during its remarkable growth since 1935. He visualized some kind of permanent Penguin Trust, and he and I had a few exploratory conversations on these lines with members and officers of a few of the major Trusts and Foundations. But no proposals seemed to be apt or practicable until a promising scheme was outlined by Professor Richard

Hoggart in 1967. It secured the sympathetic interest of Lord Goodman who developed it in some detail and discussed it at length with Allen. The basis of the proposal was that a group of universities should, so to speak, collectively 'adopt' Penguin's and thus give it a measure of more permanent security, particularly after Allen's death.

To this end a new holding company composed of several universities and colleges would be created, and to this company Allen, who was the principal shareholder, would sell his 700,000 shares at something like two-thirds of their current market value, a price which would obviously make the new company a very attractive proposition to the universities. Another big block of shares held by family trusts might also be sold to the holding company. The management of the firm would continue as before, and the new holding company would have no say in editorial control, although two or three of its members could be asked to serve on Penguin's Board, and Allen would continue to be Chairman of Penguin's for as long as he was so minded.

The meetings to hammer out this proposition under Lord Goodman's chairmanship were attended by such authoritative university people as Professor Sir Alan Bullock (then Vice-Chancellor of Oxford), Sir Roger Stevens (then Vice-Chancellor of Leeds), Lord James (Vice-Chancellor of York), and Professor Asa Briggs (Vice-Chancellor of Sussex). Others who showed a lively interest in the proposal included Lord Butler

(Master of Trinity College, Cambridge). The purpose and structure of the operation were acceptable to all who participated in these discussions. But there was one point which was to prove a stumbling-block. Everyone accepted the necessity that the university shareholders of the new holding company should pledge themselves not to sell the bargain shares they were buying from Allen so as to secure a quick profit. But such an undertaking could not be a permanent commitment to future generations of university administrators. It could be binding for a limited period —three years perhaps—and there could be the further safeguard that any university which wanted to sell its shares should be bound to offer them to another shareholder in the holding company. But even this would not ensure the continuous safeguard of a university consortium as the parent company of Penguin's, and Allen's sacrifice of his valuable shares might in the long run be in vain.

Allen came to the conclusion that the plan, so attractive in essence and principle, was not the long-term answer to the problem of conserving his empire intact. By this time his fatal illness was getting its grip on him and that, too, may have been a factor in the mood of disenchantment he developed about the transfer. I don't know. The real truth, I think, is that the university scheme was the last in Allen's long series of flirtations with the future, and I believe he would in any case have decided against it. Even if the safeguards had been more effective he would never have let go. He was always in a cleft stick in these issues. He earnestly wanted to see his firm's future assured, but he never wanted to abdicate.

The Final Solution

He had to die before this problem could be resolved, and the Penguin Board then decided that the final solution of the merger with Pearson Longman was in the best interests of the firm. The irony is that Longman was the publisher Allen had taken to most in earlier years, the firm which had always been the front runner in the long, long flirtation, and there had been established a number of joint arrangements, mainly distributive, between the two firms. When he died the most insistent problem was how to finance the further expansion of Penguin's progress. The Longman solution was probably the best answer, for it promised to ensure the growth and security of Penguin. I am not, perhaps, as confident of this as I was at the time, for within two years of Allen's death three of his four brilliant senior editors have left.

Allen was right when he said in an interview in *The Times* shortly before his death that 'very few publishing firms survive the death of their founder in recognizable form'. This has certainly proved true of Penguin's. One sees, with hindsight, that the firm was ultimately bound to change after it went public in 1961, when the share issue was over-subscribed 150 times. Henceforth it was a lucrative property in City terms and therefore vulnerable to mergers and take-overs. The major holding is no longer in one man's hands, and about seventy per cent of the equity is in the hands of Pearson Longman which is controlled by a vast industrial and banking conglomerate. Penguin's is not dominated any more by its founder, and is now wide open to the winds of change. It is a prospect which an old-timer like me can't help wishing didn't have to happen. For me the Penguin image can never be the same again. The missionaries have gone and the merchandisers have taken over.

The Chatterley Case

One of the most memorable landmarks in Allen's career was the prosecution of Penguin Books in 1960 for publishing the unexpurgated edition of D. H. Lawrence's *Lady Chatterley's Lover*. The Board's decision to publish it was founded on what we regarded as solid grounds. We believed that the recent Obscene Publications Act of 1959 was a more liberal statute than any of the earlier efforts to deal with the subject. It specified that a book had to be 'taken as a whole', and not in isolated passages, before it could be condemned. It laid down the important proviso that there could be no conviction if it were proved 'that publication is justified as being for the public good on the ground that it is in the interests of science, literature, art or learning, or of other objects of general concern'. And it allowed witnesses to be called to testify on this qualification. We considered, and so did our legal advisers, Rubinstein, Nash, that under the terms of this Act we were justified in publishing, and that the Act would protect us effectively. We were encouraged, too, by the fact that the book had been published successfully in the U.S.A. in 1959.

We had been active for years in bringing this great novelist a wider audience, and in 1950 we had published simultaneously ten of his novels in very large editions. We had produced all his novels, in fact, except *Lady Chatterley*, and we thought it would be appropriate to bring it out in the seventy-fifth anniversary year of his birth and the thirtieth of his death. Our decision to publish it was a matter of principle which Allen cherished deeply.

The usual procedure followed by the Director of Public Prosecutions in such cases is to instruct the police to buy a copy of the suspect item from a bookshop and very frequently, therefore, the bookseller is also a defendant. As he usually cannot afford the costs of the litigation he pleads guilty, with the result that the book is withdrawn from sale everywhere. That, of course, is the procedure which makes the prosecution happy. We decided not to involve the booksellers, and we withheld supplies from the bookshops when we heard that a charge was being discussed by the Director of Public Prosecutions and his advisers, the Senior Treasury Counsel.

We then reminded the police that, in law, 'publication' can mean simply that one person has handed the book to another, without involving the book-sellers at all, and we told the police that they could have a dozen free copies of the book if they called at our Holborn office to collect them. And this they did at a brief ceremony which I attended. The subsequent prosecution was launched under an Act 'expressly designed' as Mr C. H. Rolph has observed, 'to inhibit prosecutions of this very kind'.

Depravity and Corruption

The judge at the Old Bailey Trial, which lasted six days, was Mr Justice Byrne, soon due to retire, and the prosecution was led by the Senior Treasury Counsel at the Old Bailey, Mr Mervyn Griffith-Jones, QC. He began by quoting from the 1959 Act on a point which was in fact one of several weaknesses in that Act, viz.: 'The book is deemed to be obscene if its effect . . . if taken as a whole, [is] such as to tend to deprave and corrupt persons who are likely . . . to read it.' The jury's first decision, he said, must be to say whether the book had a *tendency* to deprave and corrupt persons likely to read it. Mr Griffith-Jones tried hard to make sense of these loose phrases in the Act, but the difficulty about them, of course, is to define any clear-cut meaning of a *tendency*. How can you define a 'tendency'? How can you measure it? How can you generalize about it when some people might have it and others not? Mr Gerald Gardiner, QC, had a very apt comment to make on this business

Allen Lane's earliest editors: Eunice Frost and Alan Glover.

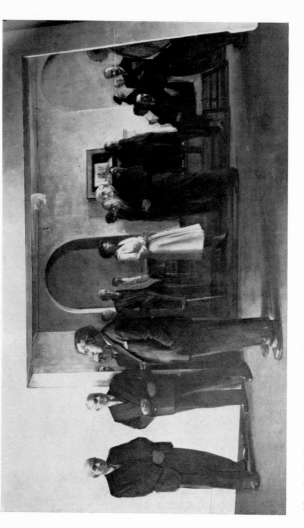

After the Conference: The Penguin Editors, a painting by Rodrigo Moynihan, R.A. (1955). From left to right: Dr E. V. Rieu, Sir Allen Lane, J. E. Morpurgo, R. B. Fishenden, Sir William Emrys Williams, Richard Lane, Noel Carrington, Miss E. E. Frost, A. W. Haslett, A. S. B. Glover, Professor C. A. Mace, Michael Abercrombie, of becoming depraved and corrupted. 'Nobody suggests that the Director of Public Prosecutions becomes depraved or corrupted. Counsel read the book: they do not become depraved and corrupted. Witnesses read the book: they do not become depraved and corrupted. Nobody suggests the judge or the jury become depraved or corrupted. It is always somebody else; it is never ourselves.' He might have touched on another aspect of this depravity and corruption nonsense. It has class-conscious undertones; it implies that depravity and corruption are more likely to occur among the lower orders than among their betters. What else could be the implication of Mr Griffith-Jones's question: 'Is it a book you would wish your servants to read?' It was during this difficult exercise that Counsel dropped his first clanger. 'Would you approve', he asked the jury, 'of your young sons, young daughters—because girls can read as well as boys—reading this book? Is it a book that you would leave lying around in your own house? Is it a book that you would even wish your wife or your servants to read?' This last old-fashioned question, alas, merely made the jury smile. The ineptitude of these remarks was to be frequently echoed as the prosecution laboured on.

Although the Act insists that a book on trial for obscenity must be judged 'as a whole' and not on selected passages, Mr Griffith-Jones, in his opening address, appeared to ignore this proviso. 'You will see on page 7 . . .' he told the jury—but he got no further when Mr Gerald Gardiner (as Lord Gardiner then was) for the defence rose to object. First of all, he said, the jury must read the whole book, and not until that essential condition had been observed would it be proper for the prosecution to put questions about any passages in the book. Mr Griffith-Jones demurred on this vital point, but the judge accepted it. The members of the jury were given copies of the book and sent off to a comfortable room on the premises to read it. The last of them finished his task on the third day, and then the court proceedings were resumed.

No Witnesses for the Prosecution

There were some odd features about the case. The defence called thirty-five witnesses to testify to the merits of the book, including such distinguished authorities as E. M. Forster, Dame Rebecca West, Dame Veronica Wedgwood, Roy Jenkins, MP, Norman St John-Stevas, MP, Lord Annan, Stephen Potter, Cecil Day Lewis, John Connell. The prosecution called one solitary witness, Inspector Monahan of Scotland Yard, the policeman who had collected the copies of the book from the Penguin office and subsequently served the summons. The Inspector informed the Court that the present case was the second one under the new Act, and that the first one had been the case against a London guide to prostitution called *The Ladies' Directory*! Lady Chatterley, it seemed, was to be put in her place. It seemed incredible that the Crown should be unable to rustle up a solitary witness to support its contention that *Lady Chatterley's Lover* was an obscene book. The only man who said so in this six-day trial was the Treasury Counsel, Mr Mervyn Griffith-Jones. It seemed a preposterous travesty of justice, and that impression grew day by day as prosecuting counsel tried vainly to undermine the authority and the credibility of thirty-five distinguished and articulate witnesses. This imposing phalanx of witnesses for the defence was brilliantly examined by Gerald Gardiner and Jeremy Hutchinson, and they had no difficulty at all in coping with the maladroit cross-examination. Although the Act said the book was to be considered as a whole, Mr Griffith-Jones seemed to rely on the interminable quotation of selected passages and on counting the number of times each four-letter word appeared. He never seemed to recognize what Lawrence was trying to do in revealing the nature of love and sex in this searingly honest book. He harped so constantly on the theme of adulterous relationships as to give the impression that the trial was a divorce case against Lady Chatterley. Mr Justice Byrne seemed to take a similar view and to be preoccupied in the main with the theme of 'adulterous intercourse'.

At one point Mr Griffith-Jones summed up his view of the book by saying, 'I mean a man running off with another man's wife. It is just that which is happening throughout this book. The whole book is about that subject, is it not?' The judge in his summing-up leaned apparently toward the same imperceptive conclusion, and the glosses he offered upon the evidence of several of the witnesses suggested that he had failed to see the case as anything more than a trial for adultery.

After the jury had returned its verdict of Not Guilty Mr Gerald Gardiner applied to the judge for costs on the ground that Penguin's had so fully co-operated in the desire of the prosecution to have a test case. Their co-operation, in fact, had cost them about £13,000, but Mr Justice Byrne abruptly rejected the application.

A Case that should Never have Started

We were all happy about this legal vindication of our decision to publish *Lady Chatterley*. Although all the directors of Penguin's were indicted in the summons, Allen bore a special responsibility, and he worried a good deal during the lengthy procedures of preparing our case. A verdict of Guilty carried heavy penalties—an unlimited fine and a prison sentence of up to three years. It was a good case, brilliantly conducted by Gerald Gardiner and Jeremy Hutchinson, and amply fortified by our train of witnesses. Penguin's got a most sympathetic press, and the whole affair did our prestige a world of good. It was, though, a case that should never have been brought, and the responsibility for launching it was too great to have been decided by Treasury Counsel. As long as their power to prosecute is dominant they may make their flat-footed mistakes again; but it was significant that when Allen decided to print a paperback of *Ulysses* in 1968 to commemorate his jubilee of publishing there was no sign of concern from the Director of Public Prosecutions. The Chatterley case was certainly a monumental landmark in Allen's long pilgrimage. I have recorded it in some detail because it meant more to Allen than any other occurrence in his life as a publisher. It vindicated the firm's reputation.

Back to Vigo Street

An event which gave Allen acute satisfaction in the closing years of his life was the opportunity to acquire the office where he had served his apprenticeship in publishing—the premises in Vigo Street where John Lane's famous Bodley Head had operated for so many years. It was far from spacious but it certainly had character, and John Lane had been given permission to make a doorway from his chambers in Albany into the Vigo Street office. When Allen heard that the old place was on the market in 1966 he promptly acquired it, before he had really decided what use it would be to Penguin's; but after some rapid thinking it occurred to him that there was a project already under discussion which would match this opportunity of a nostalgic return to the old home where, incidentally, he had scratched his name on a window-pane over forty years ago.

This is the point to mention a mercurial and controversial figure whom Allen recruited in 1960. This was Tony Godwin, a successful bookseller, whose status was not at first clearly established. He was employed originally on a vague consultancy basis; then he was the Fiction Editor and by 1965 was Chief Editor and a member of the Penguin Board. The project which Allen at first decided could be set up in Vigo Street was one which had been fostered by Tony Godwin. It was to create a hardback subsidiary, so that Pelican authors in particular could have the pleasure (and profit) of being published in hard covers as well as paperback. For several years, indeed, we had published some Pelicans in both forms, for college libraries, in particular, preferred hardbacks to paperbacks. There were drawbacks to this dual procedure, and there was a case for separating the operations. Moreover, authors were increasingly inclined to make it a condition of writing a book for us that it should also appear in hard covers, and quite often we had arranged with another publisher to include the hardcover edition in his list. But this course was not wholly satisfactory, for some publishers wanted a cut of the paperback earnings as well as their hardcover earnings.

Tony Godwin was, then, pressing for a hardback Penguin-owned subsidiary and when Allen told him about the Vigo Street acquisition he assumed that this would be the base for the new project. But at this stage Allen went off at a tangent and revived a scheme which had been on and off in his mind for some years. This was to set up a publishing house for producing elegant (and expensive) books of prestige value. This proposal, of course, bore no resemblance to Godwin's plan and could do nothing to realize hardcover opportunities for our more important authors.

But Allen was insistent. He must have a new imprint for publishing titles of a kind and in a style quite different from Penguins or Pelicans. He wanted to renew John Lane's reputation at The Bodley Head as a publisher of 'fine books' in a lavish form. The new subsidiary would be called 'Allen Lane: The Penguin Press'; it would be his own particular pet, a hobby almost, an indulgence which he believed he deserved as his jubilee of publishing approached.

Godwin accepted his disappointment and agreed to accept an alternative for which he had no heart. He reckoned it would be a couple of years before the new enterprise could be all set to go. But Allen was in a hurry. He wanted action, and he wanted to see results within a year. This was, indeed, a grievous burden for Godwin and for many others. It involved a new budget, new production problems and an editorial policy totally different from the existing terms of reference. The inevitable consequence of these hasty requirements was that the new subsidiary got off to a shaky start. The early volumes were, indeed, elegant enough in appearance, but some of the titles were by no means worthy of the expense of their elegance, and the innovation was losing money.

Clashes at the Top

The pressure under which the project was launched widened the rift already developing between Allen and Godwin, and the firm became once more torn by dissension. There were other episodes which made the difference between Allen and his Chief Editor intolerable to them both. Penguin's had in its time published with great success the books of international cartoonists—Peter Arno, Heath Robinson, Charles Addams, David Low, Searle, Thurber and many others. In due course Godwin made a deal for the celebrated French satirist Siné, with an introduction by Muggeridge, and the book was published. Allen did not care for Siné's idiom; its Swiftian anticlericalism roused in him dismay and dislike. When it came to a vote on the Board, however, Allen acquiesced, but a month after publication, and after a few protests from some 'influential' people, he told Godwin that he had decided to suppress it. The method he chose was to get all the remaining copies collected from the warehouse after dark and burned on his farm. The book was then recorded as 'Out of Print'.

To be back in Vigo Street gave Allen comfort and pleasure. When his fiftieth year in publishing was celebrated in 1969 he was fêted in a big way—functions at the House of Commons, Stationers' Hall, the Garrick Club and so on. But the one in which he took far more delight than in any of them was a little champagne party he assembled at Vigo Street for about a

dozen cronies and colleagues he had known for thirty
or forty years. It proved a most delightful and touch-
ing reunion.

The Shadows Deepen

Allen's last three or four years were shadowed by a
good deal of anxiety about business matters. The firm
was fundamentally sound and successful, but it was
plagued by frictions and clashes of temperament.
1966 and 1967 were the most unhappy and anxious
years of Allen's life in publishing. Some of the current
figures in senior management were pushing policies
which he disliked and distrusted. Among these were
promotional gimmicks of a kind Penguin's had hither-
to resisted, such as an expensive party for journalists
in Berlin to celebrate the publication of Len Deigh-
ton's *Funeral in Berlin*. Allen found himself at cross-
purposes, too, about the cover designs of some titles.
Such differences as these created tensions which shook
Allen badly, and split the management into factions.
A vortex of disunity developed in the firm. The
differences between Allen and Godwin became irre-
concilable, and the maverick Godwin had to go, with
a handshake which was, indeed, golden but otherwise
very limp. There were other resignations and dis-
missals in the senior échelon of management. Allen's
buoyancy and resilience were not as effective and confident as they had once been, and for the first time in
my long friendship with him I was becoming aware

that he had had enough, and was ready to contemplate withdrawal from the hurly-burly. Several of his letters in those years echoed the same sentiment as this one:

> The Old Mill House,
> West Drayton, Middlesex.
> Tuesday October 4th, 1966.

My very dear Bill,

Tomorrow you will be seventy, and this letter brings you all my good wishes.

I well remember your fiftieth birthday in our drinking days, and I've always regretted that I wasn't with you on your sixtieth when you were away on one of your Unesco capers in Paris.

I'm sorry we won't be seeing each other to-morrow, but I much look forward to one of our nights out a week today.

I found my fiftieth birthday a sort of 'sound barrier' the crossing of which made a difference to my thinking. For the first time I began to have doubts about my immortality.

My sixtieth not only confirmed this doubt but in fact made me realize that I was indeed a mortal.

As I approach my sixty-fifth I have decided to take some action to ensure that I make the most use of my remaining years, and to this end I now work only on three days at the office and spend the remaining four at the farm.

I find that I am increasingly intolerant of the

pace and noise of city life and increasingly drawn to the peace and quiet of the countryside.

In this I am sure that we are completely *d'accord* and I hope that we may spend many contemplative days together in the years to come.

Love,
Allen.

The Fatal Illness

Allen's final illness began in July, 1968, when he had a major operation at Middlesex Hospital for cancer of the bowel. I saw him and heard from him a good deal while he was in hospital:

Middlesex Hospital, W.1.
4.30 p.m. Wed. 28th August, '68.

My dear Bill,

I'm thinking of you now on your way to the warmth and sunshine of Lake Como. I can't tell you how much I have appreciated your visits to this rather dismal cell. Having enjoyed rude health up to the present time it comes a bit hard to face some of the problems of mortality.

At the same time being on one's own for fairly long stretches gives one a chance of reflecting on one's life and working out a plan for the years that remain.

Here I feel that we are on parallel courses, recognizing the limitations which nature is imposing, we are determined to enjoy the next phase as much as we have its predecessors.

I've had just on fifty years of city life, and that is enough. Now for a bit of peace and quiet. Not that I haven't enjoyed the half-century to the full. I have, but the time has come to give up the daily struggle, to drift with the stream.

There's a new crisis on at Harmondsworth, but I'm far enough away to feel detached from it. I think perhaps the tiredness which comes over one after a go like this acts as a protection against involvement.

I'm now due to go down to the Dr Who department.* I must say I won't be sorry when all this is over.

My love to you both,

Allen.

When he left hospital he went to Priory Farm for several months, a period broken only by his jubilee celebrations in the spring and summer of 1969. His achievement was hailed by many appreciative articles, interviews and broadcasts, and in the Birthday Honours the Queen made him a Companion of Honour, her own personal accolade.

Throughout the summer of 1969 I often went to see him at the farm. Sometimes he was back in bed again after a fresh setback; but often we spent hours

* This is what he called the radiotherapy department where he was having treatment.

in the garden drinking wine and talking over the innumerable experiences we had enjoyed or endured together. He was frequently in great pain, sometimes submerged in depression. But I never remember a time when he failed to produce a good measure of gossip and gaiety. I often felt that he was cheering me up, and not the other way round.

I believe that we both came to regard these meetings as being as good as any we had ever shared. His companionable qualities were never visibly dimmed by his illness, and we had both had a long experience of each other's values and attitudes of mind. I realized in the spring of 1970 that our long friendship had not much longer to last, and I was also poignantly aware that it had for so long given us both a profound and unique happiness. He died on July 7th, 1970. His ashes were taken to St Nectan's church at Hartland in Devon, where they lie with those of his mentor, John Lane of The Bodley Head.

Allen had fulfilled a magnificent mission. He had created a publishing revolution of international significance, and enhanced the reputation of Britain as a democratic cultural world-power. In the process he had given some of us the opportunity to share in what he created, and it is for that privilege we shall remember him.

INDEX

INDEX